You Know I Love You

Just Because of Who You Are

Jiaqi Kan

Archway Publishing books may be ordered through booksellers or by contacting:

Archway Publishing
1663 Liberty Drive
Bloomington, IN 47403
www.archwaypublishing.com
1 (888) 242-5904

ISBN: 978-1-4808-8640-7 (sc)
ISBN: 978-1-4808-8641-4 (hc)
ISBN: 978-1-4808-8639-1 (e)

Print information available on the last page.

Archway Publishing rev. date: 12/19/2019

The Book Belongs To:

_____

You Know
I Love You
Just Because of
Who You Are

Even if You rarely share the
enjoyment with me.

Even if You rarely respond me when I call your name.

Even if You rarely make
eye contact with me.

But you know that
I LOVE YOU.

YOU are the most IMPORTANT part of my life.

YOU are the most Sparkling in my world.

You Know I LOVE YOU,
because YOU are exactly who YOU are.

Thanks to...

My younger sister, Lora Lang, gave me the genesis of this picture book. She is a sensitive girl, sharing some similarities with a child with special needs. You know I love you, even if I am not around.

For almost five years, I have been studying the Special Education. There are so many people work for helping, supporting and encouraging the children and their families with special needs. They are really loving and commendable.

At last, I am most grateful to my boyfriend, Jian Dong, for his constant support of my studying and the whole life.

Jiaqi Kan

About Author

Jiaqi Kan is a graduate student major in Professional Educations in Western University. She always loves reading the picture books and believes the "power" of the picture book. Her hope is to tell young readers to know there is always a person loving her/him.

Printed in the United States
By Bookmasters